Everything about this bo[ok] time demands, wracked b[y] and one messages they hear. Fathers need help. This book will provide it. As a longtime friend and coworker of David Drury, I can vouch for his faith and preparation. His words will encourage men to embrace the highest call of their lives . . . fatherhood.

—MAX LUCADO, pastor and best-selling author

From the first word in the introduction to the last page is like getting on a fast moving train of hope, ideas, and laughter, wrapped in honesty and transparency. I work with David and see the spirit of the words lived out daily. Finally, a book about being a dad while one is in the process of being one! *The* book for all generations.

—JO ANNE LYON, General Superintendent,
The Wesleyan Church

An old publishing dictum says that men don't buy books. Tumble that dictum with *Being Dad*, now my first port of call into the father-son relationship. David Drury has written a masterpiece of tact and tenacity, a probing of parental interplay that offers exquisite flashes of insight and inspiration into the "my father" and "Our Father" relationships.

—LEONARD SWEET, best-selling author,
professor (Drew University, George Fox University),
and chief contributor to sermons.com

Being Dad is solid teaching—not just about being a dad, but a family. As the busy father of two adult children, the message of making time for, having fun with, and being intentionally supportive of your children is one I can never hear too often. David Drury's book makes me wish I had another arm so I could give it three thumbs up.

—MATTHEW SLEETH, MD, author of
24/6: Prescription for a Healthier, Happier Life

In *Being Dad*, David Drury has given us wonderfully illustrated, practical insights that every father at every season of life can apply. The highest calling and greatest gift any of us could give our families is being this kind of dad.

—STEVE MOORE, president, Missio Nexus, author of *Who Is My Neighbor? Being a Good Samaritan in a Connected World*

I love this book! David Drury has painted a compelling picture of what it's like to be a good dad, using engaging stories and experience-tested principles. The fact that it's based on the real life of David and his dad makes it even more powerful. No dad is perfect, but we can all be a little better. This quick read will encourage you to be the best dad you can be!

—DAN REILAND, executive pastor, 12Stone Church, Lawrenceville, Georgia; author of *Amplified Leadership*

One of the biggest issues our country faces today is fatherhood. David Drury has written a timely book on the art of being an "intentional" dad. I think dads of all backgrounds will find the wisdom presented here to be a great resource.

—ALVIN SANDERS, EFCA associate executive director;
author of *Bridging the Diversity Gap*

Parents, pundits, and politicians have all said we are experiencing a fatherhood deficit. David's personal and intimate reflections of the power of his father's intentional and loving investment gives me hope. As a man who experienced a similar relationship with his own father, I know this type of relationship is life-forming. As a pastor and father of two boys, I know *Being Dad* is not just a book, but a calling.

—GABRIEL SALGUERO, pastor, The Lamb's Church of The Nazarene, New York City; president, The National Latino Evangelical Coalition

In *Being Dad*, David Drury challenges himself and all dads of his generation to be the kind of dad God calls each to be. Using humorous and serious anecdotes, he captures some of the pivotal moments in his life when his own dad used his "dad role" to disciple David to become the man of God and dad he is today. As a longtime friend of David's dad, I can promise you the absolute authenticity of the relationship that he writes about with candor and creativity. I believe God will use this book to help guide the dads of this and future generations.

—TOM ARMIGER, CEO, World Hope International

Filled with beautifully written stories about his own dad putting in the love and effort it takes to be a good father, David Drury's *Being Dad* is a lovely encouragement to all dads to celebrate their children's successes and actively help them to learn from their mistakes. *Being Dad* is one of the most well-written, sincere, inspiring, and practical books I have ever had the honor to endorse. I would highly recommend this book to any father, grandfather, or dad-to-be!

> —NANCY SLEETH, author of *Almost Amish: One Woman's Quest for a Slower, Simpler, More Sustainable Life*

Read this book. You won't be sorry. Then get ten copies and give them away to people you want to bless. Three reasons you should do this. First, you won't be able to put it down. Second, you won't find more down-to-earth, engaging examples of godly fatherhood principles than the ones David gives you here. Third, a strange thing will happen by the time you get about half-way through the book. A sense of the nobility of fatherhood will begin to slip into the corners of your heart unbidden and almost unnoticed. David doesn't really tell you that's what he aims to do in this book, but that's what he does. In a world that seems to know less and less about the true and simple goodness of being a real father, this little book will restore your faith. Read the book. It's that good.

> —DAVID WRIGHT, president, Indiana Wesleyan University

I always pick up a book on fathering with a bit of trepidation . . . like many dads, wishing I'd done something more or different. David neither pulls punches nor takes cheap shots, but offers a hope-filled call to intentionality in "being dad."

—WAYNE SCHMIDT, vice president, Wesley Seminary, Marion, Indiana; author of *Ministry Velocity* and *Power Plays*

In this simply succinct yet sagacious book, David encourages a creative but critical balance between the responsible father who disciples and disciplines and the responsive dad who listens and laughs. Both are love, and both require presence. As David reflects on these issues, he invites men to consider how they can be better dads on purpose, together, according to God's desire. Men get one chance to be a father-dad, to teach character before career, by living it out with their children. If they do, they will not only be better men, father-dads who one day become friends with their kids, they will leave a "heritage of those who fear [God's] name" (Ps. 61:5). *Being Dad* is an essential contribution toward that glorious end.

—CHRIS SEIPLE, president, The Institute for Global Engagement

David Drury shares his experiences and wisdom on a topic that is so desperately needed today. *Being Dad* reflects his solid upbringing, the heart of a spiritual leader and a cool dad. This book will help individuals to grow in the declining art of fatherhood.

—CARLOS L. MALAVÉ, executive director, Christian Churches Together

A father-son relationship stands at the heart of Christianity and humanity. In this engaging book, David Drury explores this relationship first from a son's perspective and then from a father's view. Examining what a good dad does, Drury then illustrates the lessons behind such actions. Entertaining, witty, and thought-provoking, this fast-paced book will expand your horizons about what dads do and what being a dad means.

—BOB WHITESEL, author of *The Healthy Church*; professor of missional leadership, Wesley Seminary, Marion, Indiana

What an inspiring, life-changing resource! In a time of confusion and fear about fatherhood, David Drury hit a homerun! In *Being Dad*, you will find a refreshing, practical, and non-threatening book about fatherhood from the perspective of a son with an intentional dad. You will laugh, reflect, and be shaken to be a better man at home with those who call you "dad."

—IRVING A. FIGUEROA, lead pastor, Iglesia Wesleyana de Guaynabo; adjunct professor of leadership at Wesley Seminary, Marion, Indiana

David Drury is full of insight. Over the years, I've enjoyed interacting with him, musing with him, laughing with him, and reading his work. I have been a fan of his dad, for even longer. I consider him a long-distance mentor not only in leadership, but also in fatherhood. I can hardly wait to devour this book.

—TIM ELMORE, president, GrowingLeaders.com

David and his brother, John, were small boys when their father and I regularly met as accountability partners. I saw firsthand his extraordinary creativity and intentionality as a father. In addition to all the ways he loved and trained his sons, he gave his boys another priceless life gift—the example of a passionate husband, who daily loved, honored, cherished, and partnered with the bride of his youth. You're about to be blessed by a baton-passing book straight from the epicenter of a rare home where this father and husband did things right. Countless lives around the world have been inspired, equipped, and launched by his unusual influence as a teacher, leader, discipler, author, and mentor; but this book is about his greatest intentional legacy: as a world-class "dad"! Thank you, David, for generously and eloquently sharing your priceless dad-sightings and insights with us all.

> —DWIGHT ROBERTSON, founding president and
> CEO, Kingdom Building Ministries

In his easy style, David moves us through stories of his dad and lessons David has learned on parenting. The importance here is on dads being present, which is the most important characteristic that all of us can model in parenting. Just being present in the lives of our children speaks volumes. We like David's style and would encourage every dad to read this book and to be present, active, and involved in the lives of their children.

> —JIM AND JEROLYN BOGEAR, authors, *Faith Legacy:*
> *Six Values to Shape Your Child's Journey* and *Faith Legacy*
> *for Couples: Seven Values to Shape Your Marriage*

being dad

being dad

david drury

wesleyan
publishing
house

Indianapolis, Indiana

Copyright © 2013 by David Drury
Published by Wesleyan Publishing House
Indianapolis, Indiana 46250
Printed in the United States of America
ISBN: 978-0-89827-753-1
ISBN (e-book): 978-0-89827-754-8

Library of Congress Cataloging-in-Publication Data

Drury, David.
  Being dad / David Drury.
     pages cm
  ISBN 978-0-89827-753-1
 1. Fatherhood--Religious aspects--Christianity. 2. Fathers--Religious
life. I. Title.
  BV4529.17.D78 2014
  248.8'421--dc23

                              2013024664

To Max, Karina, and Lauren. I pray I'll be
a double portion of this for you.

contents

acknowledgements

May I thank those who did more than a little to help this little book exist?

Kathy and the kids continue to be tolerant of that moody man in the home library who snatches their daddy-time away from mornings, evenings, weekends, and sometimes even vacations, all so he might write books they don't read. I'm not a perfect father—but together with you I think we're the perfect family.

Steve Moore, Dennis Jackson, Dave Horne, Dan Seaborn, Adam and Christy Lipscomb, John Drury, and

Pete Yoshonis have first of all been parents I emulated, and later on were the trusted friends whose insights improved this book.

I work with a visionary, tireless team called the Executive Cabinet of The Wesleyan Church. I also have the privilege to admire the private character that makes Jo Anne, Russ, Jim, Wayne, Kevin, and Dennis parent (and grandparent) so very well despite their complex and pressured lives.

An untested and unpublished writer told Kevin Scott about a quasi-memoir manuscript on fatherhood which he had hid away in an attic for years. Kevin never failed to believe in it, and for that I'm grateful. Publishing a book for men isn't considered good business these days. Good thing Wesleyan Publishing House isn't just a business, and has ministry on the mind more than money. I'm thankful to Craig, Jeff, Rachael, Lyn, Jaymie, Susan, and the whole WPH team who have co-crafted and creatively championed a dozen different writing projects we've partnered on over the last five years.

Of course the rest of this book could be considered one big thank you to my father. Thank you, Dad, for all that follows in this little book which adds to your large legacy.

introduction
being dads together

We were standing by one of those high-top tables at a bar in Boston telling stories. Bill and Jared were good storytellers. We laughed hard. We started to tell stories about our fathers. Some were funny, others intense. Many times, when I started sharing stories about my father, my friends would say, "I wish I had a dad like that." Both Bill and Jared said that a few times this night.

After one of my final stories, Bill stared at me for a long, uncomfortable moment. Jared and I both knew that Bill's CEO-father was largely absent in his life. He knew a lot *about* him, but he felt like he never really *knew* him. In many ways, Bill represented so many guys from my generation. We wanted to be good dads some day, but we were usually trying to do it completely *different* than our own dads. Many of our fathers didn't leave enough to imitate.

I am a part of the generation of self-taught men. We learned manhood from our peers or heard about it secondhand from our mothers. Because of this, we often abandoned notions of manhood and fatherhood. We are a generation of men who taught ourselves to tie a tie, or rather, ditched them altogether. We are the ones who taught ourselves to shave—or just grew haphazard beards instead. Our mothers taught us to ride bikes. Our sisters taught us to be manly. Our girlfriends taught us to make out. And some of us have even had to learn fatherhood from our wives. I am in that generation, but I am not of that generation. Thus, the stories.

Bill finally broke the silence: "Dave, you should write a book that tells stories about your dad. I'd love to read that and learn what it's like to be a good dad. I don't have any idea what it will mean to be a good dad, and I need someone like you to share what your dad did and why he did it." Bill was dead serious. He told me to write a book about fatherhood from the perspective of a son with an intentional father.

So I wrote this book.

I hope that by hearing the stories of what my father did and drawing principles from them, you and I can make the ideas our own—and we can become better fathers together. You see, when I started this book I wasn't yet a father myself. I am not some experienced super-dad who does it all right and wrote this book to make you feel guilty. You may have seen books like that—where the author peers from the back cover in his tailored suit and tilts his chiseled chin just so in a way that says, "I can make you a man like me."

This is not that book. I am an untested and incomplete father. My kids are still very young now, and when I wrote most of these words, my wife was pregnant with our first child—so I hadn't done anything worth preaching to you about. This is not a book about how awesome I am. I am not the hero of these stories.

I do, however, write these ideas on fatherhood with the best experience on being a dad one could have. I have a dad. In that sense, all men can be experts on being dad. The journey toward intentional fatherhood starts with learning from what our fathers did or did not do.

I risk that oversimplification because it is crucial to start there and not miss out on what we can learn. This is a book about being dad on purpose. Our own childhoods can be the canvas on which we paint our own intentional fatherhoods.

There are a few things you should know from the start.

we are on this trip toward better fatherhood together

Two of the greatest barriers to becoming a better person are guilt and fear. We should not feel overly guilty about the past or fearful about the future in this process. I don't write these pages as a "successful" father. I write them as a largely inexperienced young man who desires to be a successful father, much like most men want to be, whether in our dreams of our future or because of a very present reality (such as a pregnant wife who looks ready to give birth to triplets). We can override guilt with a new hope as dads. Let's face our fears with the courage to pass on a strong legacy to our children.

being a dad is also about manhood

This book is not necessarily for women. If you're a woman, feel free to read this to better understand and support the fathers you know—or to process your own childhood and your own father-experience. But hopefully you will give it to the father of your children for him to read. (He's the guy over on the recliner watching the game.)

As for you men, understand that part of being a better dad also means becoming a better man. Much of being a dad on purpose involves tapping into our instinctual manhood and the stories we experience or hear that teach us about it, things that sound a little bizarre to women. That's because, believe it or not, some men on hunting trips can actually get a little teary-eyed if they think about these things long enough. This is even more likely if he is sitting alone with his dog in a pickup truck.

you are not your dad

While we can all learn from our dads, we are not trying to imitate them. Part of being a dad is starting new traditions and creating new realities for the next generation. What I'm saying is that if your dad was more like Homer Simpson than Bill Cosby, don't worry. You can break the cycle for your own kids and start fresh. In the same light, those of us with exceptionally good fathers must also seek out our own type of fatherhood without just rehashing what our daddies did.

i'm a Christian and i see being a dad through that perspective

I'm an ordained minister. Think of it this way: What father wouldn't be proud to have his son grow up to be a "man of the cloth." We ministers don't have the credibility or status we used to have in this world, but it's still a more preferred career path than motorcycle gang member. Regardless, you should know from the start that while I don't come off like a religious zealot and over-spiritualize everything, I do believe that we can never become the dads we really want to be without the help of God in our lives (see chapter 5). So while few chapters touch on the idea, there is a crucial spiritual factor to being a dad like you want to be.

my dad was not perfect — no dad is

I'm not writing a book about being a nice person. If so, I would write about my mother. She's a much better *person* than my dad. If you met them both you'd probably like her a lot more than him — most people do. In fact, if I was born a girl, I would be writing a book right now called *Being Mom*. But I'm not a woman, and I can't become a mother. So I'm not struggling with how to be a mom. I'm wondering how to be a good dad. If you're a man, I bet you are too. Even if you don't have kids, this subject is probably important to you as you seek to intentionally invest in the next generation. My dad was a great dad, but he made a lot of mistakes, and he's still making them. I don't agree with all he did or does today. There are a lot of things about him I'd rather not adopt into who I am. Making those kinds of decisions is all a part of becoming your "own" man. The reality is that you don't have be a superhero to be a good dad. Intentionality is 99 percent of successful fatherhood, and apathy is the reason for every father who fails at the job. It's not about your skills, education, or upbringing. It's about being a dad on purpose.

"dad" is the most important name you'll read in this book

I never mention my dad's name in these pages. I don't need to. To those who don't know him, the stories and ideas found here stand on their own and could be applied to your own father, or the way you would like to be as a father. To those who do know him, these stories and ideas only add to the remarkable figure you have heard of or know well. To me, he is simply, and incredibly, Dad.

Visit beingdadbook.com for more information, resources, and writings on fatherhood connected with Being Dad.

part 1
the early years

The presence of a father in the early years is not only important for practical reasons, but also for the way a child will see the world for years to come. As fathers, we have the opportunity to shape the way our sons will understand their own masculinity, how our daughters will understand the opposite sex, and how both will approach God. Young children are so very moldable, and more often than not they match the mold their fathers make for them. Here are some stories about how my father molded me, and how you and I can intentionally do the same for our kids.

dad on tape
making the extra effort

My dad often traveled for his job when I was young. His work required a lot of speaking and out-of-town meetings. As a kid, though, I just knew Dad was gone and didn't really know the reason why. Along the way, Dad decided that enough was enough, and put a yearly limit on his overnight trips. Once he reached a hundred scheduled nights away from home in one year, he capped it, and people would have to schedule things for the following years. As a national and even international speaker and writer, this was a great career restriction not many would make, when the average for his peers was 150 or more nights away.

Even with that travel cap, I would miss Dad when he was gone. Mom was always there, rarely leaving town without me, but as a kid, it was hard to see why Dad would have to leave. It was hard to go to bed without him reading a story at night.

Being a nice, little, church kid, my favorite book to have Dad read was *Bible Stories for Little Eyes*. Dad knew this, and one day before a trip, he gave me a tape. It had stories he had read from that book and recorded for me to listen to. Each night when he was away, I would pop in the tape and listen to Dad read my favorite stories as I followed along in the book.

Now, I wasn't a completely stupid kid, I knew Dad wasn't there. And it wasn't better to have Dad-on-tape than Dad-in-the-flesh. Why did this mean so much to me as a child? As most parents know, kids can occupy themselves without our help. Even if we cancelled some business trip to L.A. to spend time with them, they might spend the whole weekend playing with what we can clearly see as senseless and exponentially expensive toys. Don't they know that we sacrificed for this quality time?

The principle is one of *effort*. Kids want to know that Dad is making the effort to be with them, love on them, and be proud of them. Children can read a dad's effort long before they can read words. There are three common problems that hurt our effort reputation with our kids. We need to make sure they don't read these on us.

earning a good-effort reputation

teaching instead of ignoring

Many times we think that if we ignore our kids long enough they'll "get the picture" and let us read the paper, watch TV, or talk to a friend on the phone in peace. As you may have discovered, not only does this not really work, but more importantly, kids read right through it. We don't want to teach our kids to interrupt for petty reasons, but the first few times a kid says "Daddy, Daddy, Daddy, Daddy, Daddy, Daddy, Daddy, Daddy" while we're reading might be a good time to quietly teach them not to interrupt, rather than just ignoring them, or worse, telling them to shut up.

explaining rather than excusing

This is a huge trap for us busy dads. The worst part is that often times we do have a good excuse: Life is busy, and the kids should know that sometimes they don't always get what they want. The problem is that this response teaches our kids that we're not able to manage our lives and that "circumstances beyond our control" make it impossible for us to be with them. This frustrates kids, and it's also not entirely true. And looking at it from the kid-perspective, it makes a dad out to be a wimp—a man who just can't control his life and schedule to do what he *really* wants to do. We should tell them the truth and explain life rather than excusing it away.

being present rather than making promises

It's not just empty promises that are harmful. It is true that nothing breaks trust like a promise that becomes a lie. But all promises, even those kept by a dad, can be harmful. The problem resides in the need to make promises in the first place, not in whether we can keep our word or not. If we are making promises to our kids, then we are trying to placate them because of some frustration, fear, or desire they have. It is better to figure out just what that frustration, fear, or desire is in them and talk about that directly. The tough part about figuring out what those are is that their real problems are often with us, and deep down we know it, and thus avoid it. We need to suck it up and love them, not just promise to love them at a future date.

In my home, I honestly never felt like one of the things Dad had scheduled around. I knew I was the priority. Even when he was gone I knew he had made the effort to be my dad all the time.

I still have that tape of Dad reading my favorite stories. I wouldn't trade it now for its weight in gold. It's a priceless souvenir of his effort to make me the priority of his life. Your intentional effort—no matter how seemingly small—can create a priceless "I'm the priority" feeling in your children.

dad think:

questions to ask yourself or a group of other dads

This chapter says, "Children can read a dad's effort long before they can read words." What extra effort are you already making as a dad that is making a difference?

What were the most common excuses you heard from your parents growing up? Do you use some common excuses?

What kinds of things do your kids do that you'd rather just ignore?

What excuses do you think you use the most? How can you rephrase these in the future?

Do you agree that promises can be a problem as a parent? How can you help your kids feel like they are the priority?

the dirty glass
loving like the Father

When I was a child, few things were so essential to the identity of being a dad than mowing the yard on Saturday. For a little boy emulating his father, this manly pursuit came behind driving a truck and shaving with a razor. Seeing my dad mow the lawn one hot Saturday when I was only a toddler inspired awe in me. To see him working so hard, likely clad in the 1970s Saturday uniform of cut-off jeans and a sweaty red T-shirt, made me want to do something special for him. A drink of water to quench his thirst seemed to be perfect.

This may well have been my first attempt at retrieving a glass and filling it with water from the faucet. Having come straight from playing in the mud by the garden, I childishly forgot to wash my little hands before grabbing a milk-blemished glass from the dirty dish pile our house, like every house, had by the sink. Flipping the one-armed bandit of a faucet distinctly to the hot side of lukewarm, I filled that glass to overflowing for Daddy. Wobbling out to him at the mower, shouting, I suppose, for him to stop and have a drink, I held up that rare present to him as if it were a cup full of diamonds. At that point, Dad had a decision to make.

response vs. reaction

A father must daily make decisions on what a child's actions deserve in response. Teaching, stern advice, correction, pride, encouraging words, praise, laughter, punishment—these and hordes of others run the gamut of parental response options. But when our children take certain actions, we often respond too quickly. Perhaps we as fathers should not think as much about what *we* need to do in the situation, but rather, what our *kids* need from us.

Every action of a child is deserving of the right response rather than the flippant reaction we often choose to make. Let's be straight with each other: When our kids do stupid things, it ticks us off, and we immediately think, "I need to pass along some sense to this kid." But, as we intuitively know, when our kids *do* something, it often means they *need* something. Reading what kids need is the greatest skill any dad can develop. And giving them what they need in response is the greatest gift any dad can offer. We must respond to them rather than simply reacting to them. When we are tempted to react too quickly, we should first "read what they need," and then respond as we know we can.

the big gulp

Looking down at his earnest son holding up that milky, dirt-floatie-filled, distinctly warm and cloudy mess of a drink, my father had one of these reaction/response decisions to make. In a moment that is telling of more than just the moment, Dad seemed to not even notice the glass. What he saw was his boy extending flawless kindness to his father. What he saw was his child's desire to thank his dad for his hard work and his son's great hopes of making his dad proud by bringing him a drink without any help in getting it or in knowing he needed it. What he saw was not what he needed to quench his own thirst, but what I needed to satisfy the daddy's pride-shaped hole in my little chest. Dad grabbed that glass and knocked it back like only dads seem able to do. Whether he remained thirsty, was gagging, or was grossed out I don't know. What I do know is that experience explains what a father can be to his child.

our Father

But that is also what God can be to us. We as the children of God long to thank him for his work. And I believe the desire is in us all—no matter how religious we are. We want to do our best somehow. We extend our milky, dirt-floatie-filled, lukewarm lives to him because of who he is. When we do that, he doesn't even see the dirty glass of our lives; he sees in our eyes the love my dad saw in mine. God sees what we need, not what he deserves.

Living that example of God's nature is one of the greatest treasures a father stores up while raising his children. Kids always seem to tie their view of a Father in heaven with their fathers here on earth. This is a huge responsibility, but a relatively simple one. We don't need to be perfect as dads, but we can extend our own dirty glasses to God and to our kids. My bet is they won't even notice our dirty glasses. They'll be looking into our eyes just like we're looking into theirs.

dad think:
questions to ask yourself or a group of other dads

Do you have high expectations of yourself that you have trouble living up to?

What kinds of things do your kids do that you have trouble reacting too quickly to?

How could you respond to them instead?

Do you have a cute story of something your kid did for you that made you proud? Explain.

How are you connecting with God these days? Do you think he'll accept you as you are?

the stolen moustache
humbling yourself

It wasn't a big deal. The owners of the store had changed many times since the early 1950s. I didn't even know why a kid would want to have a fake moustache as a toy. How lame and old-fashioned! The thing only cost $1.25. It was no big deal at all.

But to Dad it was. Here he was, a forty-year-old man going back to his hometown with his wife and kids in tow, walking into the former J. J. Newbury department store and telling the manager, "When I was a kid, I stole a fake moustache toy from this store. I want to apologize

for that and repay you for what it would be worth today."
You can imagine the strange look the man gave him. It
wasn't a big deal. Even I knew it wasn't a big deal. Why
humiliate yourself after all these years over something
that cost no more than a candy bar?

To prove a point, that's why.

pride and humility

Every dad is and can rightfully be a tad prideful. A
dad should be a rock for his kids. Dad is an unswerving
force for the world to reckon with. Dad is a man big
enough in ego for his kids to brag about on the play-
ground. But every dad needs to face a moment in which
he shows his kids that he is not perfect. But the key is
being a big enough man to face it like a man. Dad
engaged in this simple restitution act to show my brother
and me that very principle. He was a man with a good
sense of pride and destiny, but he wasn't so full of himself that he couldn't humble himself in front of his kids.

We didn't have our hopes that Dad was perfect
dashed against the rocks that day. Instead, we knew from
that day on that Dad was a big enough man to admit he

was wrong and do something to correct it. Even if it seemed like no big deal!

finding the balance by focusing on two goals

As dads, we want to emulate this humility. Finding the right balance is the tricky part. None of us as dads want to be weak pushovers around our kids, especially when it comes to admitting we're wrong. That's tantamount to crying over spilled milk for Big Bad Dad. We also don't want to be prideful jerks who never let our kids see us crack. Some of us had that kind of dad. Holding up that kind of image fakery severs communication lines and passes along the wrong torch to our kids. We want to be dads who are strong enough to give our kids a sense of security, but humble enough to connect emotionally with them, as imperfect people just like them. If we keep those twin goals in mind, we will be a lot closer to getting there.

a sense of security provided by dad's confidence

The key to making this a reality for our kids is our consistency. There's nothing that communicates safety like a dad who is in control of the situation. And there's nothing that ruins that security like a dad who is out of control. Oftentimes, we dads try to act or look tough in some way, but because we look like we're out of control, our kids actually end up with less confidence in us. Consistent confidence in doing what's right is what those who come behind us want to see in us.

an emotional connection created by dad's humility

What is interesting about this issue is that it flows from the first. When a dad humbles himself and apologizes to his friend, wife, or even kids, the little ones somehow see that Dad is still in control. In a way, Dad becomes someone who is still right even when he's wrong. If we think in this way, we may start to apologize all the time for no reason and get hooked on it! Try it sometime—instead of covering for yourself or giving some fake excuse to your kids, try humbling yourself for a change. I promise it'll be great. That is, as long as your wife doesn't faint when she sees you do it.

dad think:

questions to ask yourself or a group of other dads

Do you have a story of stealing something as a kid that you still remember? Share.

When have you said you were sorry for something big?

On a scale of one to ten, how difficult is it for you to humble yourself and say you're sorry? Why do you think this is?

How good are you at being strong enough to give your kids a sense of security?

How good are you at being humble enough to connect emotionally with your kids as an imperfect person?

monster night
goofing off

There's nothing quite like wrestling with your dad if you're a little boy. I've heard some dads say that if they're gone for a week, they have to spend several hours on the carpet with their kids just to get the wrestling worked out of their system from their week hiatus. Whatever the reason, there's something very physical to the father-child relationship.

Every week for several years my brother, father, and I would have what we deemed "Monster Night." This name arose from Dad's peculiar ability to glare at us in a distinct way, tipping us off that he was morphing into a monster that would chase us around and wrestle us until we were wheezing with equal parts terror and joy. The nights usually followed a simple formula. Mom would be out of the house for her weekly women's group or a class she was taking toward a degree. After she was gone for a bit, lights would begin to go off in the house, and my brother and I would know the time had come. We would scurry around in circles and then find hiding places, which, considering all the "SHHhhh-ing" and "Where is he?"'s, were about as secretive as a firecracker in a funeral home. Dad would find us in short order, after circling the hiding spot a few times, slurping and groaning like a monster, playing dumb to our obvious location.

Once we were found, my brother would make his great escape to his room, where he would hunker down, who knows what for about fifteen minutes in monster-slaying preparation solitude. Then Dad would drag me out to the living room, tickling, wrestling, and giving me noogies till I was red with laughter. In a flash, my brother would then reappear in a full superhero-special-agent-western-gun-slinger outfit complete with a cape and a briefcase full of spare plastic guns and fighting accessories. He would run into the room, sometimes launching off a couch or chair, flying with his arms out and landing square on the center of Dad's back with both knees acting like photon torpedoes to the monster on top of me. Wailing in true pain, Dad would invariably be vanquished, and we boys would run away to our next pseudo-hiding place, and the cycle would continue. It is a wonder Dad never needed major spinal column surgery.

becoming a goof off

Despite all of the training we men went through in high school or college, goofing off is hard to do once you're "Dad." Giving lectures, imparting advice, and teaching lessons—these things seem to come naturally for all parents. It's like we flip on some over-the-hill switch when we become parents and start to say things we've never said before—sometimes even eerily sounding like our own parental units. What really sets dads apart from one another is not the time they spend disciplining their kids, but rather, their ability to effectively goof off with their kids. Good humor and fun times aren't just needed by our wives; kids need them too! In fact, they're needed more by our kids than our wives. They've heard and seen all our jokes and tricks a thousand times by now anyway.

You can almost always spot a fun dad in a crowd. His focus is on giving a good time to his kids. Because of his wacky ways, he's a virtual clown even if he's wearing Dockers and a Polo shirt. He's the one making faces to his four-year-old in the middle of the Walmart checkout line. He's the one doing the fake separated thumb trick for the tenth time on that vacation to Florida, and the kids still trying to do it themselves in imitation of him. He's the one playing hide-and-seek in the mall while his wife rolls her eyes, knowing she's got one more kid to straighten out that night.

It's funny how the simple things a dad does make the most lasting impressions. You never quite realize them as a man until you start doing them yourself. Passing along these experiences makes life more enjoyable for the kids, and in reality, for us too. Every man wants to be a kid again deep down inside. Having kids is our chance to be a kid again, while also giving the kids a chance to have the time of their lives growing up.

dad think:

questions to ask yourself or a group of other dads

Did your dad do anything goofy or fun with you when you were a kid? Explain.

What's the last goofy or fun thing you did with your kids that they loved?

What fun traditions do you lead your family in?

On a scale of one to ten, how fun do your kids think you are? Why?

What fun ideas could you list here that you plan to do with your kids soon?

the saved block

encouraging the spiritual quest

The children of well-known spiritual fathers often ride a curse into this world. High expectations, suspicion of favoritism, and the "PK" (pastor's kid) label often drive children to rebellion by their teenage years. We often see it coming when they are still small kids. How many of us have rolled our eyes when thinking of some conniving, little, pastor's kid who seemed to get away with everything? For a father who has a spiritual influence, position, or even occupation, this struggle will be the greatest in helping his children form their own identities without going off the deep end. I was a child in just this type of situation, with a father in an influential ministry role. Because of that situation, one night helped my spiritual development more than any other.

july 21, 1980

Like many kids brought up in the evangelical church in the 1970s and 1980s, I attended transitional churches that still had regular altar calls. One week we even had children's revival meetings with altar calls every night. Monday night of that kids' week, I walked down front to consciously make a decision to follow Jesus Christ. I went home that night with good news for Mom and Dad.

My father was once asked when he met the Lord, or "became saved." He responded, "Well, that's a hard one to answer. It's as if you asked me when my dad became my father." After pausing he concluded, "My Father was always my Father." I don't believe he meant this as a comment on when a person really becomes a Christian, but more as a comment on how the whole process felt for him. In the great legacy that was passed from my grandfather's family to my father's, I had many of the same feelings when it came to my spiritual quest. God had always been a part of life. Every bedtime story or prayer contained biblical teachings or spiritual requests. Every meal included thanks. Every Sunday involved services. In many ways, I experienced the same "always been" spiritual experience that my father described in response to that question. When people ask me when I was "born again," I often think of answering with the time-tested joke, "I was born at an early age."

We are more than the sum of our atoms. And any relationship between father and child must deal with more than the physical and emotional people our kids are. We must involve ourselves in their spirit as well.

When I came home that Monday night in 1980 and told Dad of my spiritual landmark, he didn't brush it aside like so many other decisions a seven-year-old might make. He treated it with respect and told me he was proud of me. But instead of having a long talk with me about what it meant, he took me in the garage, and we made a little piece of wood with the saw and router. We put the date, 7/21/1980, on this block of wood. I knew what it meant, and so did he. It may seem a bit trite, but for over thirty years, I've escaped doubt of my salvation in Jesus Christ because of that simple block of wood my dad took the time to make *with* me. Encouraging that decision and helping me grow through the years enabled me to know even as a child that I was not faking it. It was real. It was mine! I didn't suffer from the nagging question of whether my faith was independent of my family—because that date was my date and no one else's.

spirit guide

A dad can be the strongest spiritual force in a child's life. It doesn't matter if we think women often find it more natural to talk about such things. It isn't an issue of simply talking about your "spiritual side." Every father has his own spiritual way of life. *Every* father! We don't have to copy some spiritually well-known leader to be the person God wants us to be. We should be ourselves with God. And most essential to our journey in these pages, we must be ourselves with our kids. Being a dad on purpose is living our spiritual lives so our kids can see them. Whatever it is that you do to connect with God, be sure to show your kids you're doing it. Whatever they are growing into, encourage it, and help them become themselves in God. We fathers can be authentic spirit guides for our children. In fact, if we take fatherhood seriously, we *must*.

dad think:

questions to ask yourself or a group of other dads

What kind of spiritual lives do you want your kids to have?

In what ways are you already successfully modeling that kind of life to them?

How could you show them your spiritual side more?

When is the best time of the day or week for you to pray with your kids?

What kind of spiritual milestones in your kids' lives could you more intentionally celebrate in the future?

seesaw prioritization
walking the family talk

There are significant times when we are children that we don't fully understand until we are adults. We cannot process their full meaning until many years have past. This goes for positive as well as negative experiences. We often assume that children react more emotionally than adults to stressful or happy events. This is often not true. We figure this out when we see a son continue to play joyfully with his toys when told that his grandfather just died, as though nothing of significance has happened. We figure this out when a daughter doesn't thank us for some great thing we have done for her, as though your massive sacrificial deed was insignificant. This is not to say that such things do not radically affect children. In fact, those seemingly unaffected children may be brewing rage, thankfulness, fear, joy, or frustration without even our most discerning eye detecting it. These emotions often surface as children mature into adolescence. Many have studied and commented on how this affects kids with intensely negative experiences, such as abused children. But what about those kids with intensely positive experiences? Do those emotions percolate over years, only to surface down the road with a parallel intensity? I suspect this is true, because it has been the case for me.

putting your priorities where your mouth is

My father experienced several years of surging popularity among his peers in his ministry setting. With surprise to our family, Dad found himself nominated for the top denominational position in our church government. This in and of itself was not that earth-shattering. There are always those nominated to such posts who are put there to either pad the ballot with obvious non-electable yet respectable people, or to show others who are not likely to win that they are appreciated—a kind of public commendation for a job well done, short of an elected promotion. Most democratic governmental systems work this way. But because of his fairly wide appeal—in spite of his relatively young age of forty-two—Dad came out with the most votes. A majority had not been reached, but most likely the swing votes from the next ballot would decide the outcome.

What happened has marked and will continue to mark my view of Dad with increasing intensity. He stood before the conference's delegates and spoke of us—his children—*first*. Then he spoke of his career *second*. He articulated how these years were pivotal in our lives, and that we needed a father who would be around more than that top position could ever allow. He withdrew his name from contention. He torpedoed his moment of greatest praise because of his priorities. He sunk the ship that was his surging career on the day it came in. But it was his family was in the boat that most concerned him.

I didn't quite understand all that was going on at the time. But what happened in the ensuing days marked me even more. Mom and Dad didn't even tell us of his decision, as far as I can remember. I heard it from others, especially old men. These elderly retired ministers with their hearts speaking to their own past lives would walk up to me in the halls of that convention center and tell my brother and me that they greatly respected our dad. They told us that he did a great thing. They told us we were lucky to have a dad like that.

As telling as the ones who spoke were the ones who did not. There was a glaring absence of those my dad's age speaking to me. Years later I discovered why. They were not admirers of him. They didn't want to be like him. They didn't want to give similar speeches. Instead, they thought he was foolish. They thought he had a duty to the denomination. They thought he made a mistake. I've talked to several who questioned his decision because he, as they say, could have done "so much more for God" had he been in that position than he has done since.

Our quaint quote on the perfect vision of hindsight has become our great disclaimer for lives lived without discernment. Old men tend to be the only ones who know anything about fatherhood, and for them, it's too late to do anything but offer discounted wisdom. As has often been said, no man lies on his deathbed wishing he had spent less time with his kids and more time with his career. We would like to take the advice of old men. We want to learn from the inadequacies of our fathers. We want to become the dads our kids want to have, not the very least dads we think they need. Many of us want to put our priorities where our mouths are. So how do we actually do it?

authentic prioritization

My father corrected a false presumption for me early in life. He taught me that pie-charting my life is a dangerous endeavor. Mapping out our spiritual, vocational, familial, emotional, and physical lives into percentages doesn't do justice to authentic prioritization. No one can divide every day into neat little time categories and keep it the same forever. Different times in life call for different things. He instead used a seesaw illustration to explain the family and work balance of life. Every dad has a playground-style seesaw in his life. On the one side is his family; on the other side is his work. His job is to stand in the middle of the board and feel out what kind of balance is needed. The effort goes into making sure that neither side slams the ground or gets thrown off the ride.

The key to thinking this way is responding to what is needed rather than imposing some preconceived action onto our families, jobs, or any other part of our lives. Being a dad on purpose is more about responsiveness than responsibility. What are our kids' needs at this phase in life? How will our decisions affect them at this time? What exactly do they need from their father at this age? These and other questions will help us to prioritize in an authentic way. It centers our fickle pie charts on their priorities, not ours. And if we dads are honest, that is what we want to focus on anyway.

Once we are being these kinds of dads, we won't need long to make the right decision for the phase our families find themselves in. My dad didn't need a lot of time to make this major career decision. It was who he had become prior to the day of decision. Let's prepare ourselves in being dad on purpose in the same way.

dad think:

questions to ask yourself or a group of other dads

How do you feel you are already prioritizing your family in an authentic way?

What feels more urgent in your life than family and oftentimes crowds out the family priority?

What do you think your kids need you to respond to right now?

What is unique about the stage of life your kids are in for the next five years as compared to their lives?

What are the implications for them when it comes to the major life decisions you might have coming up in the next five years?

when i grow up
treasuring their future

Yes, I grew up to be a minister. This is not any real shock to those who know the amount of pastors in my extended family. It's like a family business, I suppose, although not as fiscally lucrative as "So and So & Sons."

When I was just twenty-three and at my first church, my dad showed up at my house with a picture frame. I didn't recall seeing it before. It was a framed drawing I made when I was very young in response to a teacher's question, "What do you want to be when you grow up?" My crayon-clutching tiny hands had drawn a two-dimensional rendition of a church sanctuary, complete with colorful pews, church people, a Communion table, a stage, a cross, and a pulpit. I was standing behind it with arms raised, speaking to my imagined future, rainbow-colored congregation. At the top, I had scrawled, "When I grow up I want to be a minister."

Whenever I was asked that perpetual question, the answer was the same. Even though my dad had never been the pastor of a local church in my lifetime, I felt a strong draw toward church ministry all my life. With this virtual certainty in his hands that his son would be a pastor, Dad still resisted the temptation to pressure me into it. Perhaps that is why I never questioned it. Even when considering college, the choice was in my hands, and though he rationally explained the benefits of the ministerial program at the Christian school I ended up attending, he never mandated I go there and would always couch his statements with, "If you go there, they have this and that, but it's your decision completely."

It is the joy and duty of a father to treasure his child's potential. Being a dad on purpose is making a kid's future the purpose of the present. There are several things that demonstrate to our kids that we are not only interested in what they will become, but that we already can see them becoming it as well.

treasuring their future

being proud vs. being derogatory

For most kids, the worst thing they experience growing up is being mocked or ridiculed. There is added pain when it comes from an adult, and multiplied pain when it comes from their parents. Making fun of our kids is the opposite of being proud of them. We must be proud of their future before it even becomes a reality, so that they can be proud of what they are in fact becoming, and then have the confidence to go the distance.

being admiring vs. being apathetic

Many of us as fathers have fallen into the rut of apathy when it comes to what our children are becoming. We have tried everything, and nothing seems to work. The remedy for this is simply perspective. We need to take a long hard look at our kids and see what is admirable in them. They have been woven together with some unique values and some profound purposes. The greatest remedy to our apathetic fathering can be developing into fathers who admire our kids for seemingly small qualities.

being rational vs. being emotional

It is easy for us to connect to our kids' future emotionally. This common reality is not in fact a problem, but rather, it is a strength. But when we begin to communicate with our kids about their futures in strictly emotional ways, we don't give them any of the wisdom our longer lives and fuller experiences have afforded us. We must learn to communicate rationally, even at times impartially, with our kids. They will not accept our random emotional comments about their future. They'll just roll their eyes in embarrassment. But they long for our rational wisdom and discerning eye on their lives. If we give it to them in the right packaging, they'll come back again and again for more.

being helpful vs. being hurtful

There are countless ways for a father's comments to hurt a kid, even with an unintended hurtful statement. Our thoughts on our children's futures must not make them feel pressured, stupid, or less-than-confident. We should convey to them their freedom, let them know they are competent enough to make the decisions, and instill in them the confidence it takes to make it in the world today—even when they are small children. Being even a small help for our kids' futures will make a big difference. Likewise, being even a small hurt in our kids' pasts will haunt them. Our very small actions have a very large effect—a double-edged sword that can be intentionally used or unintentionally harmful.

dad think:

questions to ask yourself or a group of other dads

How proud of your kids are you? How do you show it best?

What do you admire about your kids? Do they know these things?

In what ways are dads more emotional than rational when it comes to the choices their kids make?

What things do parents say to their kids that hurt more than we suspect?

What wonderful dreams do you have for your kids?

part two
the growth years

Our children experience growth seasons where they outgrow their pants in six months and they might even start to outeat us at the dinner table. Pretty soon they outrun us and outthink us, as the time seems to be slipping by. We wonder where the years have gone—we never thought we'd feel that way when the kids were young and screaming in the middle of the night. Those days and nights seemed to last forever. Now they seem like a blink of an eye. Here are some stories of how my father intentionally made the most of investing in me during the growth years, and some practical ways you and I can do the same.

dave's cassettes
teaching about money

I heard a prominent motivational speaker once say that he never once received an allowance. He was expected to do chores as part of his family duty. He said that he was never paid to simply be a part of the family and its responsibilities. His money would have to be earned through other work. My father incorporated a similar philosophy with us as kids. We were never paid for things that didn't deserve pay. Mom didn't get paid for doing the dishes. Neither did we. Dad didn't get paid for taking out the trash. We didn't either.

dave's cassettes

As soon as I could handle the pressure and learn from the experience, Dad began to help me dream about starting my own business. From the start, he made it clear through our discussions that this wasn't about making money, although that would be a great benefit, but it was more about learning responsibility when it came to money. With my parent's speaking schedule, my proximity and connection to other speakers in town, and the large church we attended, I decided (with great encouragement from Dad) at just thirteen years old to start a tape duplication business.

I borrowed the money from my parents to buy the first duplication machine, which was over a thousand dollars. The first month, I started the payment plan to pay them back, and well within the year, I was on my own. I would duplicate large sets of speaking tapes with a 40 percent to 50 percent markup, and once I owned a few duplicating machines outright and had a large stock of tapes, I started to turn a nice yearly profit, socking much of it away in the bank. By the time I was sixteen, I retired from my "Dave's Cassettes" business (a pretty campy name I'll now admit) and invested the money in a small rental house. The money from that income helped me pay my percentage of college costs, of which I was expected to pay an increasing, preplanned amount each consecutive year I went.

teaching our kids to fish

What a gift it was to learn so many financial principles from those years in a miniature business that rose and fell on my own money and hard work! My father proved the truth of the old adage by "teaching me to fish" rather than just giving me a weekly allowance of "fish." And when you add up several years of potential allowance, it likely would offset the money it took my dad to get me started. With this small measure of financial independence, I wasn't able to "bum" off of my parents when I needed money. I learned early that spending money to make money is the best way to save. I also learned that money didn't make itself, and that I needed to be responsible with the small measure of money I did have. During these growth years, my dad made it a priority to make a man out of me when it came to money. When I look at the financial shape my friends are often in, I don't think as much about the financial decisions I make now; more often I think about the principles I learned when I was thirteen. We must understand that being a dad on purpose is teaching our kids to be responsible with money.

tips on teaching financial principles to our kids

principles over profit

It is more important for our kids to figure out the principles involved when dealing with money than to actually make any of it. In fact, not making a boatload of money may teach them the stark reality that money does not come easily—or learning to regroup and invest their money in something more wise the next time. (Of course, in this situation, we fathers may have to pony up a second "start-up" fund.)

monetary investment over manual labor

Lots of kids have to get a job. The difference comes when kids have to use their creativity, contacts, oppor-tunities, and resources to make more money than just hard work will get them. If you want your kids to work in a fast-food checkout career forever, then an entry level "McJob" is the way to go. If not, help them see the value of investing for future reward over just working for temporary funds.

personal independence over paycheck dependence

My father once wrote a chapter in a book called "How to Get Rich Slow." In this wry title, you can see a bit of his financial philosophy. He always told me that the key to financial independence was not in how much you can make, but in how little you can spend. My Dutch wife from Holland, Michigan, was overjoyed to discover that such doctrines had been ingrained into me. It is no surprise that families are sending into the world paycheck-to-paycheck credit card slaves today. We teach these habits to our kids early, and they simply act like twelve-year-olds making a thirty-five-year-old paycheck, and spending it likewise. When a kid "borrows" five bucks from next month's allowance in order to buy candy, is it any different than a forty-year-old using a credit card to buy a motorcycle when he or she doesn't have the money for it yet? It is essential that we teach our kids to be independent with their money and responsible for how they spend it.

efficient work over easy work

Many my age remember the cartoon character Scrooge McDuck's favorite motto, said in his thick Scottish accent: "Work smarter, not harder." This was also the theme of my father's constant financial advice. Every word of wisdom spoke to doing things with more efficiency rather than simply doing things the easy, but mindless, way. My brother's entry into the same early teen, business start-up world is an example of this. Instead of simply watering every tree in his large tree farm, he put together a system of irrigation with automated controls. This way he only needed to flip a switch and everything would get watered. After adding several timed computers to the system, he could practically forget the whole business for several weeks at a time. When he sold the business in his later teens (with all the trees still in the ground) he made a ten-thousand-dollar profit! We need to teach our kids to not just "work hard for their money," as the song goes, but to work smart for it as well. I'd call a seventeen-year-old with a cool ten grand pretty smart, wouldn't you? I might even call him up to ask for some money myself.

dad think:

questions to ask yourself or a group of other dads

Growing up, what kind of things did you learn about money?

What do you wish you had been taught that you weren't?

Do you agree with each of the following claims of this chapter when it comes to teaching kids about money? Why or why not?

- Principles are more important than profit.
- Investing money is more important than manual labor.
- Becoming independent is more important than getting the paycheck.
- Kids should learn to work smarter, not just harder.

a dad's secret weapon

using positive reinforcement

When I was growing up, it seemed no 1980s sitcom was complete without the recurring theme of a bad, report-card grade. The TV kids would go to great lengths to hide, alter, or defend their grades to their parents. For most kids, this was a true-to-life picture of report-card day. Some of my friends even anticipated a spanking for their grades at the end of each term and would head home in tears. Things were quite different in our home.

Every single report-card day from the time I was in sixth grade, our family would go out for pizza. My brother (in first grade when it started) and I would have our grades in tow and, as my father would invariably say during the drive, "Tonight we are celebrating all your hard work for this term, and I'm proud of you whatever your grades are." Our grades were positively reinforced every single pizza party. We would make our parents proud with great grades, and we knew that the party at the pizza place would be all the better with good grades, so we tried our best each year.

positive rewards

It is difficult to get kids to do what we want. Children act so childish all the time, don't they? Sometimes we wish they would just grow up. The difficulty with kids is the same difficulty with adults: getting them to do what *we* want them to do because *they* want to do it. Anyone with a position of authority can make people do things. Any boss or father can use punishment to make a point, and sometimes that is necessary for both. But the higher road and more utilized choice by successful dads and bosses alike is the path of positive rewards for preferable behavior.

We all know how to do it, but more often than not we use it as the backup plan. We need to realize that people are not unlike dogs. We will go to great lengths for a treat! This is not using empty promises and desperate pleadings once a kid acts up in public. A kid in that situation probably needs negative reinforcement in a decisive manner. But on a daily and consistent basis, kids should behave well because they want to do themselves and their parents proud, not simply because they are living in fear of the consequences, which can—and will—result in them simply going behind your back to get away with things without punishment.

the secret reinforcement weapon

The largest positive reinforcement for any child is often the pride of his or her father. Being a dad on purpose is when your kid makes you proud by trying to make you proud. Being proud of our kids is our secret weapon. To know that Dad would be proud of my brother and me regardless of our grades didn't cheapen his pride of us when we did well; it bolstered it. We longed to make him even more proud. You know you're doing your job as a dad when your kids want your pride more than they want the pizza.

dad think:

questions to ask yourself or a group of other dads

Which positive rewards might have you responded to as a kid?

What positive rewards are you giving your kids already? What things do they love and are motivated by?

What kinds of things about your kids make you proud these days?

How could you better show your pride of your kids?

What are you doing that your kids might one day be proud of you for?

10

legacy trip
leaving an intentional legacy

I knew it would happen years before the trip came. I saved up money to buy souvenirs. I studied maps. I dreamed with Dad about what we would do when we got there. But the significance of my trip to Israel with my dad when I was thirteen is only now beginning to take shape for me.

Dad told me from an early age that he would take me to Israel when I was thirteen because I would start becoming a man then. It was about the closest thing to a Bar Mitzvah that a Protestant Hoosier could get. Dad told me it would be just him and me for this trip too! We would celebrate who I was becoming and make a pilgrimage to the Holy Land to commemorate it. This trip was a special event for me as I came into my own as a young man. It was a pivotal point Dad went way out of his way to make happen for me. I can look back at it today and see the intentional way he built a legacy for me.

a legacy trip

It is hard for me to think of that trip now without thinking of another father—one who heard about our trip and did similar ones of his own. Many people heard of the trip we took, and the identical one my brother took the year of his thirteenth birthday. One particular father who is a good friend of mine took big-event trips with his two children as a result. He called them "legacy trips" and even mentioned them in his heavy speaking schedule. He was the popular-epitome of a good father. In most ways, I believe he still is. But I can't get out of my mind what those legacy trips mean now. This friend of mine, who had a rapidly growing speaking and teaching career, had an improper relationship with a woman half his age and, more significantly, left the mother of his two kids. I often think of the legacy trip those two remarkable kids have been on now. It has taught me that the great Israel trip event that many people look to as an example of my dad's character means nothing in comparison to the daily legacy he has left and, by the way, continues to leave me today.

The legacy of a man is not left in a day. In every case, a legacy is not calculated until you are dead and your life can be measured in total sum. Having a few good years as a father is not the goal of any dad. Being a dad on purpose is leaving an authentic, lasting, and intentional legacy. We want to leave a legacy that not only our kids will treasure, but that our kids' kids will contemplate and carry on themselves. With this kind of lasting legacy, our family tree can expand not only in quantity, but also in quality. This will occur because of the strong legacy of roots that we are securing firmly every day of our lives. We can do this. We will finish well. We can leave a legacy that outlives our own lives. We can only finish well if our private legacy behind the curtain and beyond the limelight is more potent than the one others like to talk about.

dad think:

questions to ask yourself or a group of other dads

What are the best parts of the legacy others in your family have left you? And what's the best part of the legacy you're already leaving?

How would you define the word *legacy*?

How can you leave a more authentic legacy?

How can you leave a more lasting legacy?

How can you leave a more intentional legacy?

What events or trips could make it a more significant memory?

the beef station

discipling your kids

Christians these days talk a lot about what we call the Great Commission. The last words of Jesus Christ before he ascended into heaven amount to a job description for we Christians on earth before he returns. The core of it involves the process of going and making disciples of all nations. This is a noble goal. This is a legitimate priority. I'll step out on a limb here and say that Jesus was right.

The problem is that we're awful at actually doing this. We know this is true. That's why we talk about it so much. Christians nearly always talk the most about things we do the least. I suspect the problem lies not in programming or relevance or even intentions. Our churches today are the best ever. The twenty-first century may be the most culturally relevant times in history for the church. The amount of evangelistic books, messages, and movements has never been more prolific than today. Then why are we still so feeble at this chief goal of making disciples? I suggest it is because we haven't learned to do it with our own kids, whom we know better than anyone. How then, can we hope to transfer that process to other people?

the beef station

An old gas station a quarter mile down the road from our Indiana house had been converted into the dank, dingy, and somehow legendary Beef Station. The big red bull on the discolored plastic sign lured few newcomers to the place. Most who ate at The Beef Station were regulars. Truckers and farmers knew where the good food was. They also knew where there was enough smoke and mustiness to keep away the Yuppies. The Beef

Station was just such a destination. For two or three years after our momentous trip to Israel, Dad and I would go to breakfast once a week at this memorable eating establishment. Dad would get his black coffee, and I would get my home fries with extra ketchup, and then it would happen.

It was these breakfasts that taught me how to *be* a Christian man, not just *do* the things a Christian does. It was then that I learned the principles of the New Testament. It was that day of the week that I collected countless napkin diagrams that simplified life's spiritual principles with everyday, "real" language. It was there that I first heard the inner confessions of a father who was beginning to treat me like a man, even a peer. It was those mornings in which I was first discipled. We even called this time our "discipleship meetings." My father knew that being a dad on purpose means discipling your kids, and it was the priority of his week.

Dad discipled me the entire time I lived under his roof, but those intentional mornings together were the boot camp of my journey into spiritual maturity. Let's examine ten principles of discipling our kids that I learned from my own discipleship years with my dad.

1. Making disciples out of our kids is important enough to schedule. If we have our weekly staff meeting in the schedule, then this should be in there too. If we never miss coffee with the guys on Saturday morning or bowling on Thursday nights, then we should never miss this one either. We talk a lot about our priorities; here's a place to prove them.

2. We can't fill up our kids if we're not full ourselves. It will be tough to think about investing spiritually in our kids if we are not spiritually vibrant ourselves. As our children come to discipling age (eleven- to sixteen-years-old), we need to do everything in our power to have others invest in us and disciple us so that we can pass along that overflowing love and simple knowledge of God. And even many of us dads who aren't close to the Lord want our kids to be. So this is a good time for us to get right so that we can get our kids right. We know what to do; we might just need this motivation to start down the right path.

3. There are only weak substitutes for actually spending time to disciple our kids. This is not just quality time; it is quantity time. We shouldn't squeeze these meetings in; we should schedule around them and look forward to them.

4. One-on-one is the only way to show how important our kids are to us. This is no time to cop out by inviting other people to join us, or even to do it with the rest of the family. They will feel the importance of the time if it's soul-to-soul, just dad and the kid.

5. By applying the Bible, our kids will see its value for life. Living a biblical life is more caught than taught, and kids imitate the way their dads use the Bible in their daily lives. These meetings are the prime time to make this happen. This doesn't mean you have to learn to preach. In fact, it's just the opposite: Share the Bible with them on a simple, practical level.

6. We are making them disciples of Jesus Christ, not of ourselves. Some of us might try to use these meetings to build up some shrine to our own spirituality and personality. We have not truly discipled our kids until they no longer think of us when they think of God. We must point them to the cross, not hang ourselves on it.

7. Kids learn better through our humble efforts than our vain fakery. They see right through us when we try to fake things spiritually. If we instead try to open up and even express our insecurities spiritually, they may express their own fears, questions, and hurts. Then we will be able to grow together with our children as we guide them.

8. Being ourselves is the best way to help them be themselves. We cannot show them anything but who we are in God. It may not be a pretty thing, but it will impact them greatly just in the process. We shouldn't focus on the content or level of our spiritual lives; we must focus on the process of our investment.

9. Giving homework for both ourselves and our kids can help drive the following meeting. Simple and easy-to-complete tasks to do before the next meeting keeps the subject matter in the mind throughout the week as well as providing content for the next time we meet with our kids.

10. Cover the tough issues as much as the easy ones. These meetings are the best time to cover the issues of sex, sin, hate, drugs, fear of death, the existence of God, racism, etc. How many of us have struggled to find the right time to bring up these things, or even worse, were ambushed with an issue when we were unprepared? We can let our kids know a week ahead of time that we're discussing a tough issue, and then we have to make it happen.

dad think:

questions to ask yourself or a group of other dads

What person has had the most spiritually significant influence on you?

What are the ideal intentional things you hope to do to be a spiritual influence on your kids?

What kind of date or meeting could you schedule with your kids to make these things happen?

What do you think is the ideal age to start this?

What kind of resource or book would you use to go through with your kid? What ideas do other people have for resources?

let the saw do the work

making parables out of work

At times I felt like it was my father's mission in life to never let me sleep past 8:00 a.m. on a weekend. Every Saturday of my life, it seems, a knock would sound on my door and it was time to head out and do some work with Dad. It didn't matter if we were digging a ditch or renovating a house, things always followed a simple formula: Dad and I would sweat in the sun working, my brother was the designated tool-fetcher, and every job would reach a moment of teaching.

The most memorable work parable of all came whenever we were using a handsaw to cut a piece of wood. I would try to cut it and the jagged blade would catch and jump and wobble and do everything but cut the wood. Dad would then gently say, "Son, let the saw do the work." I believe I heard that phrase from him more than a thousand times in my life. Interestingly, only about half of those times came while actually using a saw. The other times were moments where the handsaw parable on patience applied, and it would help me through. If I just relaxed and slowly pushed and pulled the saw, the tool would cut the wood, rather than me cutting the wood.

dusty dads

A man I know once had the job of mixing feed to supplement his income. For about two weeks, each day he came home from work, his two boys, ages two and three, would look at him, smile, and say, "Boy, Dad, you sure are dusty!" He would reply, "Yes, I sure am dusty." Then he would get cleaned up. He didn't think too much of this until he was washing his car and saw his oldest son doing something very strange. He was picking up the gravel and stones that were in the driveway and rubbed them into his pants. The dad asked his son, "What are you doing?" The son replied, "I want to be dusty like you, Dad!"

Work is a mysterious domain to kids. Parents need to help their kids not only learn to have a work ethic, but also to get meaning out of work. They look at what we are doing and want to be "dusty like us." And while working shoulder to shoulder with them, we can bring parables out of the work to life.

The simple work parables my dad used weren't original to him. Guess who he heard them from? You got it: his dad. And where did Grandpa get them? Yep: my great-grandfather. I believe every dad has these little words of wisdom to give, and being creative and constant in delivering them makes the difference in passing on our wisdom to our kids. Creativity in expressing them enables our kids to remember the words of wisdom. Constancy in applying our principles to our own lives enables our kids to live by our words of wisdom.

dad think:

questions to ask yourself or a group of other dads

What are some "work lessons" that your dad or other people passed on to you when you were younger?

Which ones have you already passed on to your kids or hope to in the near future?

What other work lessons do you live by that should be passed on to your kids?

Take some time now to write your top five work lessons (from others or that you've come across). When will you begin implementing them?

the funeral home
dealing with death

In just two months, they both died. Grandpa had been ill for years . . . expected to not live long. Amputated legs, lost kidneys, heart ready to quit—these things don't make you expect a long life for an old man. But Grandpa was so bright and alive in mind and spirit. He just didn't quit—until one of his two sons died. My dad's only sibling—my uncle—had a massive heart attack at just fifty-one years old. He died so suddenly and tragically that I know several non-family members who were permanently shaken by it.

I remember being with the family at the funeral home. I stood in the corner, half-concealed by a large fake plant. My aunt was a wreck of tears and wailing. My teenage cousins looked like they were in shock, all the color drained from their faces. My parents were busy handling details. I felt, perhaps for the first time in my life, an ominous sense of the ugly presence of death in that room. I was just a few steps from my uncle's casket.

My grandfather was in a wheelchair already at this point with two amputated legs. He was wheeled up to the casket. It seemed like there was an invisible plane nobody crossed, as if there was glass covering the casket. I hadn't seen anyone break that barrier until Grandpa did. He reached his hand into the casket and carefully patted the hands of his oldest son, passed now before him. He said, "You were a good boy, and I'm proud of you." Grandpa's heart for people was amazing; he was a caring and gentle man. His body was broken in a dozen ways, but his heart seemed unfailing . . . until a few short months later when his heart quit too. All of a sudden, half of my dad's immediate family was gone.

A man in his forties searches for his legacy. He sees the men who shaped him fade into what is next and looks to make his own mark. Dad turned forty-one the year his father and brother died. His identity as a man was shaken as he dealt with death firsthand. More importantly, he came to grips with his own eventual death, and it marked him. A man must be marked before making a mark in the world, even if that mark extends no further than his children.

life and death

Dealing with death is hard for men. It is even harder for fathers. As men, we have a tough enough time with the insecurity the subject generates. As fathers, we must also deal with the position our own death would put our children in. The father-factor makes the untenable idea of death a horrifying subject not brought up on purpose.

Dad dealt with these deaths by leaving a greater legacy than he would have if they were alive today. He made his mark not in spite of death, but because of it. You see, as dads we must quickly discover that we are not invincible. We must employ our mortality as the motivation for living right in the present. Dealing with death, as I've seen in my own father, is less about grief than it is about life. The question, "How will I live without so-and-so?" eventually transposes into, "How will I live my life from now on?" We cannot simply examine other loved ones' deaths. Examination of our lives is the crux of dealing with death as a father. We ask ourselves, "Who will mourn my death? Where will my legacy be left? Why would my children feel something missing? What have I entrusted to them thus far in life?" Being a dad on purpose means dealing with death as a fact of life.

dad think:

questions to ask yourself or a group of other dads

What were the most significant deaths in your family growing up?

What did you learn about life and death through these?

Have there been any recent deaths that your kids are aware of? What could you do to help your kids understand death?

How could explaining death to your kids actually help you grieve too?

i'll never leave her
loving mom

At first it seemed a strange thing to say. Saying "I love you" or "I'm proud of you" are the things a good dad is expected to say to his kids. But there was another recurring statement that was a bit random. There was no pattern to its delivery. It seems this statement came at all times and situations. Dad didn't have any identifiable reason for saying it. The promise was unconnected to any problems that arose. He apparently felt that telling us that he would never leave our mom stood all by itself.

"No matter what happens, son, I'll never leave your mother." Why would he say that so frequently and with such intensity? I wonder what prompted all those unsystematic proclamations of his love for Mom. Maybe it was some friend of his who lived out the opposite of that promise. That betrayal may have invited Dad's desire to reassure us. Maybe it was a recent argument he and Mom had. The tiff may have caused Dad to make this statement to himself as much as his boys—to reinforce it. Maybe it was a continuing passionate love for Mom that just bubbled over from time to time. That love may have inspired the most random acts of expressing his love for Mom to us. I suspect that all these were true.

a different world?

Few doubt that the greatest single difference between the way kids are raised today and the way they were raised fifty years ago is the number of kids affected by divorce. It is now common for kids to assume their friend's parents are divorced. The parents who are still together are the anomaly, the exception to the rule. The occurrence is so frequent that we say things like, "Are your parents together?" when getting to know someone new.

Parents should be the constant in their children's lives. They should be the bedrock of the existence that enables children to feel secure and loved. Children should never have to question their parents' commitment to each other, because they automatically interpret any separation as something they are a part of; and they are right. Dads often try to justify things to their soon-to-be left children: "Don't worry, this is just between me and your mother. We both love you just the same . . . and even though we aren't going to live together any more, we're still a family." Kids see through this garbage so easily, and it amazes me that we're so convinced by our selfishness that we can't see the truth behind their teary, discerning eyes.

Mistakes in the past are in the past, and many a divorced dad has been able to be the best dad possible despite the uphill battle he faces. But divorced dads invariably come to the realization that they are starting from a mile behind the starting line. Understand this, dads, if you are married now, stay that way until you or your wife dies. It is impossible to be an effective and complete father without the team that is created by a mother and father together. Love Mom and you'll be a better dad; you'll be the kind of dad and husband a son would want to be when he grows up. Being a dad on purpose means staying with Mom.

dad think:
questions to ask yourself or a group of other dads

Who's divorce do you know of that impacted the kids in a really difficult way?

Have you gone through a rough patch in your marriage that you've overcome? Explain.

Do you think it's really worth it to stay together for the kids, as this chapter claims? Explain.

What do most people in the world think about divorce and kids?

Do you know of people who have been divorced and have made the most of it for their kids? How are they pulling that off?

the runaway tent
teaching a lesson

Most fathers have their special stuff. For some, it's the tools in the garage that are hung in the exact places they want them. For others, it's sports memorabilia that is hung in the basement. Some dads treasure their tools, books, computer, old records, or favorite recliner in the den. Whatever the case, most dads have some stuff that is prime property in their minds, and when the kids get into it, the dad either cringes to think what will happen, or outright bans the kids from touching the stuff.

In my family, backpacking, camping, and all things wilderness-related were of utmost importance. I don't remember a vacation we took when we didn't camp out in the woods or at a campground (with running water, if we were lucky). We carried packs on our backs shortly after learning to walk. And before that, we were carried in a backpack ourselves. We grew up amongst the trees, hills, lakes, mountains, and hiking trails.

So you can imagine how important all the camping and backpacking equipment was in our house. We spent far more money each year on that equipment than we ever would on eating out and going to the movies combined. One year Dad was able to buy a few tents for his office staff's retreat. These large tents were the newer (at the time) kind of pop-up tents with lightweight poles that created a great dome and a huge space inside, especially compared to our musty-center-poled-wet-edged tent that only a Green Beret soldier with no sense of smell would sleep in without complaint.

I begged Dad to let my buddy and me sleep out in a new tent in our yard one Friday night. He begrudgingly agreed, since they weren't even really his tents, but on one condition: I would not ruin a thing, and I would put it up properly and stake it to the ground so that it wouldn't blow away in the wind, as these tents were prone to do from time to time.

My buddy and I had the best time in the world in our new tent-turned-hideout, and got up in the morning and ran inside to watch cartoons and eat breakfast. When we went outside to grab our things from the tent, we noticed a big bare spot with only pale and flattened grass where the tent was supposed to be. Apparently without the weight of two boys in it, the tent—with its zipper door open—acted much like a huge balloon kite, and flew down the street. This could have been prevented by staking it into the ground like I'd been told, but alas the stakes were in a bag inside the tent, never opened, and now were having the ride of their lives inside the tent-turned-massive-tumbleweed. We frantically searched the neighborhood for Dad's precious tent, the contents of which included many other camping possessions purchased in faraway hippie camping stores in Maine or California. We never found the tent. It was either picked up by an opportunistic man with a truck, who must have been startled by the kite-like tent bopping by, or it is still blowing around somewhere in the badlands of South Dakota to this day.

the hammer drops

Dad was ticked. The instructions were simple. He knew he shouldn't have let us use the nice new tent he had just bought with his office's retreat money. And all the stuff inside of the tent was gone too! Camping stuff! Backpacking stuff! The most important stuff we owned! I was in big trouble.

But Dad didn't take it out on me physically. A spanking wouldn't make the point that needed to be made, and besides, I was getting a little old for that. I cost him a bunch of money. He couldn't just take it out of my hide and break even. So he devised a plan. We made up a large chart where certain humiliating chores would net me small payments: like fifty cents for shining his shoes, or a buck for washing the cars. I can't remember much of the work I did, but I do remember that it took me *months* to build up enough credit to pay back the hundreds of dollars I owed. I learned my lesson big time. Not only would I stake down every tent from then on, but I would also follow Dad's instructions to the letter on things, especially when it involved his beloved camping equipment!

learning long-term lessons

Being a dad means teaching long-term lessons. It is easy to try to teach lessons in a minute, as though corporal punishment or one anger-filled yell-fest will effectively sink in to a kid's mind. Sometimes the best lessons are taught when a kid is punished for a long time. Equally important, kids often forget past punishments. Some of our strong-willed kids seem to forget a punishment five minutes after they received it, doing the same thing right in front of us again. The remedy for this is a longer-term and more creative punishment, one that fits the crime, like mine did. This makes the lesson a learned one. If a kid wrecks something expensive—she should pay for it to be replaced. If he vandalizes someone's property, he should fork over multiple Saturdays to scrub and paint it. If she calls the problem an "accident," then now is the time to teach responsibility over the results rather than intentions. If he is two hours late after curfew, then think up a way for him to pay back those two hours in the most memorable way so that the next time he thinks twice about being late. We celebrate creatively with themed parties and special events—but we need to correct our kids creatively to make it count as well.

dad think:

questions to ask yourself or a group of other dads

What kind of life lessons did your parents teach you as a kid?

What's the worst thing your own kids have done recently? How did you punish them? Could there have been a more creative and lesson-teaching way to go about it?

Do you think there is validity in spanking kids? Why or why not?

What are some good ideas of ways to teach lessons to your kids?

part 3
the peer years

We didn't put all this investment into our kids so they could live under our roofs forever. We are preparing them for something, somewhere, *out there*. We don't know what it will be. We can't prepare them for everything. But we can instill in them the kind of character that is flexible to any situation, the kinds of qualities that are useful and admirable. We hope what we've done to intentionally invest in them will pay off and make them better men and women, employees and bosses, citizens and friends. Here's a few stories of how my dad invested in me during the odd peer years, including some practical ways to invest in this season when the role of a father starts to change so much, but where you and I are needed as much as ever.

cain and abel 2.0
dealing with sibling issues

Most brothers are not the kindest of individuals to one another. I've heard of brothers who physically beat up each other even into adulthood. Other brothers incessantly put down each other verbally. Some brothers fiercely compete with each other in everything. My brother and I were no exceptions to these common traits among brothers.

One time my brother, John, was so angry with me that he took a kitchen knife and carved my name into the Plexiglas door on our microwave. He apparently thought that Mom and Dad would read the huge D-A-V-I-D in the door and I would get into big trouble. Needless to say, that one backfired in a matter of minutes, once they figured out I hadn't done it. If that wasn't bad enough, another time John took a knife and started to come after *me* with it!

Before you think this was all one sided, I had my share of guilty times too. Older brothers like me are just a little smarter about the kinds of ways to get the younger ones. Sometimes I would make faces at him when he was getting in trouble, which caused him to nearly blow his stack and just get in deeper trouble. My favorite trick was to get really close to him, perhaps even draping a brotherly loving arm over his shoulder, and to whisper to him, "You're the biggest baby I've ever seen" and then run away, pushing chairs in his pursuant path and locking doors behind me. But by far, our most epic battles occurred in the backseat of our often-traveling father's car.

backseat brawls

Most kids tell stories of their dads warning to pull over the car if they don't stop acting out. We pushed things to the limit so much that I remember several times that Dad made good on the threats and actually did pull over, removing his belt right there on the interstate. We were like Cain and Abel 2.0 in that backseat (or Cain and Cain, more accurately). Having different sides as our "turf" was always the prescribed remedy by our mother. She would pull the center seat belt across the Chevy's bench seat and that was deemed the sibling demilitarized zone. You couldn't cross that line because that was the boundary. Of course, just like a wartime DMZ, that line became the source of our squabbles from then on. I would place a hand across the line in a noticeable and flaunting way, and then my brother would push a shoe or belt buckle hard into my hand and then claim he was safe because the violent incident took place on what was his side. Often he would dangle a hand over my trying-to-sleep face and say in a stupid voice, "I'm nooot touchinggggg yoouuuuu!" One of these times, I had endured enough and simply punched him square in the sternum, knocking the wind out of him so bad that he couldn't even cry effectively. The car was pulled over at the next underpass because of that one.

One time I thought I would pull a fast one on John with the whole boundary thing. I convinced him that I wanted to lay down on the floor of the car, because it was so *very* comfortable. I traded him two action figures (by the way, Dad, they are always called action figures and never dolls!) to play with for the rest of the day in order to receive this perceived luxury. So I plopped down in the gully of the backseat of that Caprice Classic, the middle of which had a horribly huge hump that had all the comforts of lying flat on the back of a moving camel. But I faked it well—even sold it by grabbing a pillow and acting like I was asleep and as content as a bug in a rug. Of course, the jealousy I had counted on in my brother began to take over. He started complaining to Mom about the situation, clamoring to get a turn on the floor of the car. Just like my devious older-brother mind had planned, he was eventually begging me to trade with him. I did, of course, after bargaining for several action figures, tapes to play on my Walkman, and all three pillows for the rest of the day.

Apparently, he was so misled by my acting job before then that he actually enjoyed being down there sprawled out over the middle hump in the car. My plan had worked flawlessly, and I stretched out on the cushiony seat with all the pleasures a grade school boy could dream of. But the big smile on John's face made me wonder if I had been double-crossed by my own plan. His contentment hadn't been a part of my equation.

stopping a sibling showdown

As you might imagine, by the time I was seventeen, this situation had become rather untenable. Even though I was done with high school and about to enter college, my brother and I were still acting like we were first graders, which was considerably more immature for me than for him, as I was five years older. It didn't make sense for me, as a six-foot-tall teenager who shaved daily, to be acting like that with my brother. But my parents were long on patience, until one trip we made out West— which was to be the last with the four of us living under one roof. My brother was going through the particularly rough years of junior high, and I was a mixture of aloofness and irritation on the whole trip. By the time we had arrived in Tahoe, Utah, from Indiana, my dad decided to have a talk with me.

Our usual antics had continued across the country, but Dad's response had not been the usual punishments or threats of pulling the car over. Instead, he just looked tired of it all, feeling his middle age. Dad told me about the tough times that John was having at his new school. He told me how much it hurt him to have me treat John poorly. He let me know that I was acting a lot younger and more immature than he expected of me. And he told me that I should begin to have an intentionally positive influence on my brother.

What he said was not quite as significant as the way he said it. He treated me like a young man, like a friend almost, who he was just disappointed in. He didn't scold me like a child; he respected me and treated me like a peer with a problem. My father knew that there comes a point when you need to deal with your children as peers. He also knew that being a dad means tackling the heart of sibling problems. From that day on, two things happened. First, I started to invest in my brother, mending the years of separation our sibling behavior had caused. And second, Dad treated me more like a fellow man, or peer, than a kid. An intentional dad must deal with these sibling issues and set the stage for each kid to become a positive influence on the other.

dad think:

questions to ask yourself or a group of other dads

Did you have siblings growing up, and if so what kind of fights did you have?

Do your kids fight a lot? Does it feel out of control at times?

How could you coach your older kids in handling these fights?

What could you do to help your kids understand how to treat each other in general?

the letter
confronting your kid

There is often a point in a person's life that one perceives as the turning point in his or her journey. Part of being a father is making sure you are there for your kids when they reach that point. Of the two roads that diverge on that day, one is usually preferable in the long run, and kids need a wise voice in their lives to help see the right path. This is true even if they choose a path you wouldn't, because eventually, they may have a chance to switch roads and your wise words way back when will mean even more after the fact.

My turning point came in college. This is not surprising to most who have entered those supposedly hallowed halls of learning, only to discover that college is often a string of pearls consisting of ping pong, movie nights, video games, all-night-pseudo-study sessions, cold pizza, risqué parties, and all forms of goofing off known to man. It is a concrete fact that sports that have no real point or goal have been invented on a college campus, from Hacky-Sack to Frisbee. Juniors and seniors often relate the meaning of the word *sophomore*, gloating that it means no less than "wise fool." If this were the case with any second-year student, it was with me, especially the second part.

One weekend that year demonstrated my foolishness in living color. My parents were leaving town with my brother, and I was commissioned to come home from college and housesit for them. This was an important job for several reasons, beyond just getting the mail and feeding our many animals on our hobby farm. My father's mother lived with us at the time, and even though she lived in an independent apartment attached to our house, she still needed a little bit of attention. I was paid for the weekend to get her paper each morning, and then spend a few meals with her, while also checking in on her throughout the day, doing things she needed done.

As many nineteen-year-old guys faced with the opportunity of hanging out in a large house with no strings attached, my wheels started turning. I made every endeavor to reassure my parents that I'd do the job well, and then I privately planned to take my college girlfriend to the house and have a romantic dinner together and possibly watch some movies as though we had this great house to ourselves. In the hubbub of picking her up from the school an hour away, and taking her back, I basically did none of the jobs I had committed to do. The animals went unfed, the mail stayed in the mailbox till the last day, and Grandma got all her papers at once on the final day. I visited her for only brief moments when coming in and out of town. I dropped the ball—big time.

Now this was a poor showing by me, for sure, but many fathers would have written it off as simple "stupid college guy" antics and kept the promised money to make a point. Instead, my dad sent me the wad of cash inside what I now call "The Letter." The letter was six, hand-written pages of the strongest language possible. Dad put the question to me simply: "What path will you choose?" He explained in the letter that my head wasn't screwed on right at that time and that I was going three or four different directions with my life and needed to shape up and become a responsible man. He phrased it all in that peer-fathering tone he'd begun to use since I was seventeen. He was not only disappointed in me, but was shocked that I would do it all without a thought of my own irresponsibility.

putting the question

I was so full of shame and guilt from that confrontation that it forced me to look inside myself for the first time in several years. Dad likely saw this confrontation coming, noting little issues in his head that pointed to a path in my life that was not the best. But he never mentioned anything until that letter, and he poured it all on in one confrontation, saying, "You don't have to respond to this letter with me—but you do have to respond with your life. Which path will you choose?" He apparently knew that being a dad on purpose means confronting your kids when they take the wrong path.

Shortly after the letter from Dad, I broke up with that girlfriend for good, threw myself into my college studies, and got a job. And a few months later, I experienced the most solid calling from God on my life that I've experienced. It was a turning point. Two paths diverged in a wood, and Dad was there with his wisdom compass. More than just being present, my dad knew how to confront his kid in a way that made a turning point a permanent change.

dad think:

questions to ask yourself or a group of other dads

What turning points did you have in your life when you were younger?

At what age do you think most people reach their turning point?

What are the signs you've seen that a kid needs to turn his or her life around?

How can a father help that transition happen?

How can you be ready to confront your kid at that pivotal moment in his or her life?

the advisor
coming to the rescue

Once I left the house, I really left the house. I didn't go back on the weekends much and didn't spend any college summers at home. I wasn't really a homebody. So on the "letting go of your child" scale, I certainly helped out my parents by never being around once I turned eighteen. In fact, my parents took all my stuff out of my old room and boxed it up, and that room became decorated with lacy, flowery things, transforming my teenage jock room into a bed-and-breakfast style guest room.

I was on my own in many ways and could handle life's problems and decisions without much help. But I was not really a full adult yet. You know the type—a tweener of sorts—who have many of the outward signs of adulthood but are still very immature in some respects. You can have a car, a home to live in, even a fiancée, and still be very much a big kid inside. This was true for me. I was to be married two months after school, and I was making one of the biggest decisions of my life, and now it would affect not only me, but also the woman I had chosen to marry.

I had been pursuing an opportunity to move to Washington, D.C. to work with a few friends who were all planning to move there to start a church and live cool, metropolitan lives that involved a lot of hanging out in coffee shops and being "authentic." The time to pull the trigger on moving was approaching, and I knew that I needed to make plans to move or do something else. The only problem was that the head guy going wouldn't make a decision. He would never nail down his plans and would never give me a date on when he was planning to go. The more I talked to him about it, the more I realized that I was going to have to move there first— with my new bride all by ourselves in a city we had only visited once, waiting for the cavalry to arrive so we could have the life promised us.

going to dad for advice

During this process, there came a point at which I asked Dad for advice. I was really searching and could go either way on the decision. The next day, Dad drove the hour to my college and took me out to lunch. He put on a different hat than normal. All the sudden he was Career Advisor Dad. We mapped out my options on a napkin like we had done hundreds of times before on many smaller issues. He helped me realize what I really wanted to do, which was move to Boston and go to school with my new wife, starting a life of our own, not dependent on my college buddies or either of our families.

Even more, Dad made clear to me after I knew what I wanted to do that I needed to quickly and decisively get out of the current plans I was involved in. He started to act a bit like a political spin doctor for me there in the restaurant, encouraging me to simultaneously resign from the project to several people, including one of my closest friends I was planning to work with. The plan included e-mailing the letter to one leader, who happened to be in South Africa, and then walking over to my friend's office and handing him the red-hot resignation letter to quit the deal. At the time, I thought Dad was totally crazy. Why go to all that trouble? What did I care if the other guy got the chance to spin it his way before I got my story out?

Only a few years later, I realized what Dad was doing—and I was glad I followed his advice. He was coming to the rescue for me. He knew that it would look really bad to back out of the team in which I had been a crucial player. He instinctively knew what was eventually found to be true—that none of the others would go that year if I pulled out, and I would be labeled as the one who pulled the plug on it in the end if I didn't crisply and simply state why I was resigning from the project in the first place. This became even more important in the following years as I worked for some of the same people who received that resignation letter.

mixed emotions

I now wonder how Dad must have felt in those weeks. Did he have that typical dad-feeling of "I need to speak my mind to him, but I don't want to influence his decision"? Did he wonder if he just needed to "let the chips fall where they may," and let me go whatever direction I chose? In the end, I believe that letting go of our children is certainly a major hurdle we dads must face. But likewise, once we've let go, it can be difficult to intercede for our children again when they really need it. In the case above and in many cases our kids face in young adulthood, they actually do need us to intercede and help them through it all. They don't need us nagging them every day about doing this or that. They need us when so much of their future is riding on their decisions. Too often we dads get it backwards, preferring to be a continual nag on the little things rather than a wise counselor when our kids need it on the big things.

dad think:

questions to ask yourself or a group of other dads

What's some of the best advice you have given your kids lately (whether they followed it or not)?

Who have been the wisest counselors in your life so far?

How could you be more like them?

On what issues do your kids take your advice as nagging instead of wise counsel?

What life choices do your kids face in the next ten years that you can be ready for?

a new best friend

reconnecting with your kids

My brother was ready to graduate from college. I was married and had my own life and career. While we still communicated with Dad often, usually by e-mail, the relationship with our dad had changed dramatically. No longer was he the constant presence in our lives of advice and reason. His voice of wisdom came only in bursts from time to time when something larger (like in the last chapter) came to a head. And even in those moments, I noticed something more like peer advice from him. His comments were always laced with pride in how we turned out that made me think he considered his job as a dad done. He had raised us and, more or less, done a good job. Now he spent a lot more effort on his work and his personal interests and hobbies. I even noticed that he talked about himself a lot more; our conversations revolved around his life changes just as often as mine.

This was a very large change to become accustomed to at first. Dad wasn't acting much like Dad anymore. As most kids do, I distanced myself from my parents a bit in my teen years, seeking to be an individual and find out my own way in life. In this process, I didn't rebel against my dad, but I certainly didn't go seeking him out all the time. Now that I reached my early twenties, I found him doing a similar thing to me. It was like he had resigned the daily task of fathering and sent me on my way, dropped like a juvenile bird out of the nest.

the right time to reconnect

Of course this was perfectly natural and actually already started by my own distancing. It did, however, make me begin to think about that relationship. Who would be my mentor now? Who would I go to for advice? Who would fill that role in my life now?

Then Dad e-mailed my brother and me and informed us that we'd now be taking father-sons trips every other year together. He'd foot the entire bill—travel, food, hotels, rental car, etc. Whatever we did would be his treat. My brother and I agreed without thinking about it long. And so began our Drury tradition of a father-sons trip every other year. We would do things such as canoe a portion of the Swanee River together or scale Ben-Nevis, the highest peak in the British Isles, and bum around Scotland together. During these trips, Dad started to treat my brother and me like something completely new: fully grown men and his peers. He knew that being a dad on purpose means letting go of his kids at the right time, and then reconnecting with them at the right time too.

a best friend

And so we became like best friends instead of just dad and sons. Because of his effort to reconnect with us as peers after our time of independence, we became friends. Now I don't feel the need to run to Daddy with every problem I have—even though he is still one of my mentors and advisors. Instead, I call him like I'd call many of my friends. We joke and converse like pals. Without any words, he gave me the sense that I was on my own and I could handle it. I was a man—not just a young man—a full-fledged adult man. In many ways, it was the first feeling of arrival in my life. It wasn't about a process he was working in me anymore. I had arrived as a man and his peer at last. Feeling one has arrived at adulthood is a perception that perhaps only a father can grant a child, and it is one granted far too infrequently to our children, which may be why we have so many adults still acting like children today.

dad think:
questions to ask yourself or a group of other dads

What part of letting go of your kids is hard for you?

What moments of letting go when kids are younger are "training" for when they finally move out or get married?

Did your father ever reconnect with you in a new way as you became an adult? If not, how do you wish he would have? If so, how did he make that happen?

What will be most difficult about reconnecting with your kids as they become adults? What part are you looking forward to?

king of the castle
knowing your changing role

Soon after moving to Boston with my wife came the obligatory first visit from Dad and Mom. My wife and I talked with them on the phone and planned their visit, discussing such seemingly trivial things as sleeping arrangements. In that conversation, Dad made it clear that in no way were we allowed to give up our bed for them. They would sleep on the floor, and that was the end of it.

Later during their visit I asked Dad why that was the case. "Why make such a big deal about it," I wondered. "It's just a bed." Dad told me that it wasn't. It was our first bed. It was our first home. It was our place, not his (even though much of the furniture was taken by me from his house, of course). He mentioned that whenever his parents visited them, they would commandeer the master bedroom; his dad would sit in the biggest and best chair and then his mom would do the same to the kitchen—as though they ruled the roost. He turned around this trend, and said that it was not their role to be anything more than polite guests in our home, living under our rules.

king of the castle

Later on I read another author who helped me realize that being a dad on purpose meant knowing that no man can be the king of his child's castle. That was the same principle that drove Dad to his dogmatic position in sleeping arrangements. He wanted it to be clear that they respected our space, our possessions, and our home. And he must have drilled Mom on it too, because it was the first time she never cooked a thing over a reunion weekend in my lifetime. Just as our home was my castle, my wife's kitchen was hers to operate the way she liked even with a mother-in-law in the picture.

Dad understood that even if we didn't yet. I came to realize over time how much freedom and pride came in having my own place that was my own responsibility. Even if something broke, it was my job to fix it. Dad would only fix something or suggest something to fix if I asked him to. Now that takes discipline for a fix-it-father!

dad think:
questions to ask yourself or a group of other dads

What kind of boundaries have your parents respected, and what boundaries have they ignored?

What boundaries would you like to set up with your kids as they become adults?

How is your changing role as a parent tied to letting your kids go? Could a problem of not respecting boundaries actually be tied to not fully letting kids go?

What things do your kids value that will likely be most important to respect their space about? (Privacy? Property? Personal space?)

the apple tree
becoming a graceful grandfather

Having grandchildren is a somewhat different experience for a woman than it is for a man. When a woman finds out her daughter or daughter-in-law is pregnant, she usually thinks, if not says, "I'm not old enough to be a grandmother!" Some men may think the same of their impending grand-fatherhood, but more likely than not, they'll first think, "Heh, heh, heh, now let's see how you deal with being a parent!" Beyond this devious pleasure in knowing that you can spoil your grandkids while changing no diapers and never having to get up in the night with a crying baby, new grandfathers also have the kinds of feelings my dad told me about.

Dad said that this was the natural way of things . . . and that his job being my dad was really mostly done now. He was a grandpa now as much or more than a father. He understood that being a dad on purpose means raising your kids to be good dads or moms themselves. He couldn't in twenty-five minutes give me twenty-five years of advice to prepare me for fathering the little baby my wife was carrying. He had to depend on the twenty-five years he spent raising me with the dubious thought that I would likely do the same things for his grandkids that he had done for me. That concept is one that encouraged my dad, because he knew he had prepared me all he could and modeled what it meant to be a dad. It is a concept that should encourage all of us. It should drive us to live every day in a way that we would have our children live someday because they more often than not will.

the fruit of an apple tree

Do you know what the fruit of an apple tree is? If you're like most people, you might respond, nearly annoyed, that it is an apple, of course. But is that the *ultimate* fruit of an apple tree? What happens after that first fruit—an apple—falls to the ground? Well, if the conditions are right, a new apple tree grows in that spot. So then you might say that the fruit of an apple tree is yet another apple tree, right? You might compare that to a father (like the tree) who has a child (like the apple), and that child grows into a fully mature adult (another tree). However, that's not the end of the story, is it? Does an apple tree only have one apple on it? Does that new tree that is planted stop the chain? No. Life continues on in an exponential growth process. Over time and in the right conditions, the final fruit of even just one apple tree can be an orchard! So that is our answer.

Your child is that first fruit in your life, but in the end your legacy will be an orchard. Who knows how many lives will flow from yours even if you have just one child? The ancient Abraham, who had only one child with his wife Sarah, ended up with such a multitude of children that God described them as the sand on the seashore or the stars in the sky when promising them to him. Today, his Jewish and Arab descendants fill the lands of the Middle East and are spread throughout the world. While you may not be like "father Abraham," if you have at least one child, you have just as much potential as he had to leave a legacy to your orchard. When a dad becomes a grandpa, things are just getting started, and an orchard awaits.

dad think:

questions to ask yourself or a group of other dads

Do you have any stories about how your grandparents or distant relatives influenced you in positive ways?

Is it hard for you to think of yourself as a grandfather? Why or why not?

How could you gracefully become a grandfather?

How will your kids make good parents themselves?

What part of being a grandparent is better than being a parent?

so, now what?

So what? So I have a good dad. So there are a lot of helpful principles we can learn from my stories about growing up with an intentional, fun, interesting, and fully devoted father. What do you do about it?

don't finish reading this book

If you're like most guys, you won't have a problem with this. Some of the chapters may have bored you to death. You started reading others while watching the playoffs of something and didn't remember a thing. If you're like most guys, you likely skipped chapters that didn't relate to you yet or are too far in your past or future to interest you now. Who knows? But even if you're an overachiever and read every word, don't finish this book. Set it somewhere easily accessible, and the next time you find yourself in a being-dad problem, pull this out and look over the contents and think through the questions in that chapter. If you have trouble connecting with your spiritual side and telling your kids about it, read chapter 5. If you need to start teaching your kids about money, read chapter 8. If you have a death in the family and don't know how to help the kids through it, read chapter 13. If you're older kid has a critical decision to make and you're not sure what or how much to say, read chapter 18. You get the picture. It's not like there aren't other ways to get help on those issues, but you (or maybe your wife) already bought the book, so you might as well get your money's worth.

breaking the cycle is simpler than it seems

If you feel like you can't get started on the path to being the dad you want to be, don't be discouraged. No matter how bad, absent, or strange of a dad you had, the cycle can be broken. You can start anew. And while it might not be easy, it is simpler than it seems. You don't have to change everything about yourself overnight. You just have to take it one day—then one year—at a time. Don't worry about whether you'll be able to handle your kids as teenagers if they are still in diapers. Just worry about the day ahead of you and being the dad you want to be *today*. Tomorrow has enough worries for itself. If you take just that first step, then in fact, the cycle is already broken, just stick with it.

talk with other dads

Get together with another dad or two or even a group and ask yourselves the Dad Think questions at the end of each chapter. You don't need to reread all the chapters, just discuss the issues. You'll learn a lot more from other dads and what they're doing, or not doing, than you will just analyzing yourself. And this kind of honest talk gives you the confidence to realize that you are already doing a good job and just need to, as my father always said, "Keep on keeping on!" I did that with a group of four or five other dads my age, going through the chapters in this book and asking the questions I wrote. It was a help to us all. While we dads met, all our children played together in the McDonalds play gym while we casually chatted, giving our wives a break from watching them. You could do the same with a group of guys in your garage, church, or small group. But trust me: going at being dads together is better than going it alone.

let your family know you're working on it

Be honest that you're trying to be a great dad but are still a work in progress. Let your wife or other supporters know first, so they can support you in the process. And then when you make a mistake, be real about it with your kids and let them know you want to continue being a better dad (read chapter 3 again if this still sounds nearly as bad as fingernails on a chalkboard). You'd be surprised at the slack your kids may give you once they realize that you're trying really hard (without it becoming an excuse for never getting better, of course).

pray

As I mentioned at the start, you'll never fully be the father you want to be if you don't come to grips with your heavenly Father. If you are a father, you are also a son two times over. Your earthly father gives you the motivation to do it yourself—and better. But your heavenly Father gives you the greatest and perfect model for fatherhood. He is perfect. He is loving. He is strong. He is your *Abba* (Father) too.

Jesus Christ is the way to get connected to God, and if you pray to him for help and guidance along the way, there is nothing he'd rather do more. Let God be your Father in heaven, and he'll equip you to be the best and only father on earth your kids could ever hope to have.